INTRO

GW00691627

The first follow⌒⌒⌒ ⌒⌒⌒ the symbol of a fish on the wall of their house. They were not just identifying themselves as Christians – albeit secretly – they were declaring the Christian faith itself.

Five letters make up the Greek word for fish: *icthus*. Each is the first letter one of the earliest creeds spelling the declaration: Jesus Christ, God's Son, Saviour. There are others scattered through the New Testament. The first apostles handed on the heart of the faith in short, memorable ways often using a question-and-answer format.

In the early Church this process of formation for baptism and for life long discipleship was called 'catechesis' (pronounced cat-eh-key-sis). The aim is to build a resounding inner echo of God's word, an image of Christ at the centre of each disciple's life through learning very simple core texts by heart.

From earliest times the Apostles' Creed and the Lord's Prayer formed the basis of what became known as a catechism: a simple and compelling way of forming disciples in the Christian faith and helping them to live out that faith with joy. The Commandments and the Beatitudes were also used from earliest times. The catechism in the Book of Common Prayer is the best known example in the Anglican tradition.

This new Pilgrim catechism – *The Pilgrim Way* – stands in this great tradition, consciously drawing on all that has gone before. It also offers something new for today's generation of Christians, helping us to understand and live out our faith and identity as followers of Jesus Christ. It is offered as a resource to help Christian people understand and grow in their faith in the conviction that the renewal and revival of catechesis is urgently needed in today' Church.

Like the very first Christians we too must know, and understand, and share and live out our faith each day.

Next page: an *icthus* symbol carved by early Christians on a wall.

ENTS

INTRODUCTION	**3**
THE PILGRIM WAY	**5**
ONE THE APOSTLES' CREED	**7**
TWO THE LORD'S PRAYER	**13**
THREE THE COMMANDMENTS	**19**
FOUR THE BEATITUDES	**27**
GOING FURTHER	**33**

Church House Publishing
Church House
Great Smith Street
London SW1P 3AZ

ISBN 978 1 78140 063 0

Published 2017 by Church House Publishing

Copyright © 2017 Stephen Cottrell, Steven Croft, Robert Atwell and
Paula Gooder

All rights reserved. No part of this publication may be reproduced
or stored or transmitted by any means or in any form, electronic or
mechanical, including photocopying, recording, or any information
storage and retrieval system without written permission, which
should be sought from copyright@churchofengland.org

The authors have asserted their rights under the Copyright, Designs
and Patents Act, 1988, to be identified as the author of this Work.

The opinions expressed in this book are those of the authors and
do not necessarily reflect the official policy of the General Synod or
The Archbishops' Council of the Church of England.

Scripture quotations from The New Revised Standard Version of the
Bible, copyright 1989, 1995 by the Division of Christian Education
of the National Council of the Churches of the USA. Used by
permission. All rights reserved.

Material from *Common Worship: Services and Prayers for the Church of
England* is copyright © The Archbishops' Council 2000-2008 and is
used with permission.

Cover and contents design by Penguinboy.net

Original Pilgrim series design by David McNeill, Revo Design

Printed in Great Britain by Core Publications Ltd. 07814 786409

the pilgrim way

Pilgrim, what do you seek?

To follow in the way of Jesus Christ.

. . . .

What is the way of Jesus Christ?

To live in God's love and enjoy God for ever.

. . . .

Pilgrim, who is God?

God is the source of all being, the one for whom we exist.

ONE
THE APOSTLES'
CREED

Pilgrim, what is the faith of the Church?

The faith of the Church is revealed in the Holy Scriptures and set forth in the words of the Apostles' Creed.

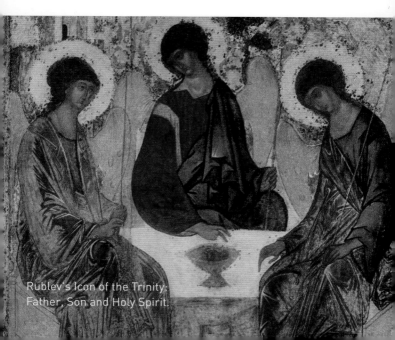

Rublev's Icon of the Trinity: Father, Son and Holy Spirit.

THE APOSTLES' CREED

I believe in God,
the Father almighty,
creator of heaven and earth.

I believe in Jesus Christ,
his only Son, our Lord,
who was conceived
by the Holy Spirit,
born of the Virgin Mary,
suffered under Pontius Pilate,
was crucified, died,
and was buried;
he descended to the dead.
On the third day he rose again;
he ascended into heaven,
he is seated at the right hand
of the Father,
and he will come to judge
the living and the dead.

I believe in the Holy Spirit,
the holy catholic Church,
the communion of saints,
the forgiveness of sins,
the resurrection of the body,
and the life everlasting.

Amen.

What does it mean to believe in one God: Father, Son and Holy Spirit?

To believe is to trust in the Father's love for the world, in the saving work of Jesus Christ on the cross, and in the transforming power of the Holy Spirit.

How do you become a Christian?

By turning to Jesus Christ in faith, by repenting of your sin, and being baptized in the name of the Father, and of the Son, and of the Holy Spirit.

What is sin?

Sin means not living according to the will of God. To sin is to fall short in our thoughts, words and deeds, through what we do and through what we fail to do. Sin separates us from God and neighbour.

What is baptism?

Baptism in water is the sacrament of new birth in Christ. We die to sin that we may live his risen life. We are washed by the Holy Spirit and become members of the Church.

....

What is the Church?

The Church is the pilgrim people of God, the body of Christ, and the community of disciples in every age in earth and heaven.

Pilgrim, how will this shape the journey of your life?

By God's grace, I will seek to understand my faith and be able to give a reason for the hope that is in me.

TWO
THE LORD'S
PRAYER

Pilgrim, how do we deepen our love for God?

We deepen our love for God through reading the Bible, participating in the life of the Church, and through worship and prayer.

. . . .

What is worship?

To worship is to lift up our hearts to God. We join our prayer to the prayer of the Son to the Father in the power of the Holy Spirit.

. . . .

How did Jesus teach his disciples to pray?

He taught them this prayer:

THE LORD'S PRAYER
(Contemporary Language)

Our Father in heaven,
hallowed be your name,
your kingdom come,
your will be done,
on earth as in heaven.
Give us today our daily bread.
Forgive us our sins
as we forgive those
who sin against us.
Lead us not into temptation
but deliver us from evil.
For the kingdom, the power,
and the glory are yours
now and for ever.

Amen.

What does this teach us about prayer?

The Lord's Prayer teaches us to praise God, to seek God's will, to ask for God's help every day, to say sorry for our sins and be forgiving, and to resist evil.

· ·

How do Christians worship together?

Christians gather to praise God, to listen to the Holy Scriptures, to pray for the needs of the world, and to share in the sacrament of Holy Communion.

· ·

What is a sacrament?

A sacrament is a pledge of God's love and a gift of God's life. God takes earthly things, water, bread and wine, and invests them with grace. A sacrament is an outward and visible sign of an inward and spiritual grace.

What is Holy Communion?

In Holy Communion Christians celebrate the mighty acts of God. Jesus had supper with his disciples on the night before he died. Taking bread and wine, he said, 'This is my body broken for you. This is my blood shed for you. Do this in remembrance of me.' In sharing Holy Communion we are nourished by his risen life today.

Why is this sacrament also called the Eucharist?

Eucharist means thanksgiving. Christians give thanks for God's grace in the life, death and resurrection of Jesus Christ.

Why is Sunday the principal day for Christian worship?

Christians worship on Sunday because that is the day Jesus Christ rose from the dead. For Christians it is the first day of the week.

Pilgrim, how will this shape the journey of your life?

By God's grace, I will be faithful
in prayer and worship,
and make the whole of my life
an offering to God.

THREE
THE
COMMANDMENTS

agohomi uis

ⲞⲀⲄⲔⲤ
HIATT
heus

Pilgrim, how does God speak to us and teach us his ways?

God teaches his people through the Bible, and above all through his Son Jesus Christ.

. . . .

What is the Bible?

The Bible is the library of books written over many centuries telling of God's dealings with the world. The Old Testament tells the story of God's people Israel. The New Testament tells of the good news of God's Son Jesus Christ, the gift of the Holy Spirit and the birth of the Church.

. . . .

Previous page: the Lindisfarne Gospels depict Saint Matthew writing his gospel, the first book of the New Testament.

21

How can we trust the Bible?

The Church believes that the Bible is the word of God. The Holy Spirit inspired those who wrote the Bible and enables the Church to understand God's word and to proclaim the faith afresh in each generation.

• •

What commandments did God give Israel?

God gave Moses these commandments:

THE TEN COMMANDMENTS

I am the Lord your God:
you shall have no other gods but me.

You shall not make
for yourself any idol.

You shall not dishonour
the name of the Lord your God.

Remember the Sabbath
and keep it holy.

Honour your father and mother.

You shall not commit murder.

You shall not commit adultery.

You shall not steal.

You shall not be a false witness.

You shall not covet anything
which belongs to your neighbour.

What do we learn from these commandments about God?

We learn that there is only one God,
and it is wrong to make gods of other things.

. . . .

What do we learn from these commandments about ourselves and others?

We learn that there is a rhythm and balance
to life and that it is holy. We learn that the
household of the family is precious, that there
are things we should not do because they harm
our relationship with God and one another.

. . . .

How did Jesus Christ summarize the commandments?

Jesus Christ says that we should love the Lord our God with all our heart, with all our soul, with all our mind, and with all our strength; and that we should love our neighbour as ourselves.

. . . .

Pilgrim, how will this shape the journey of your life?

I will faithfully read the Scriptures because they are a lamp to my feet and a light to my path. By God's grace, I will fashion my life according to the way of Jesus Christ.

FOUR
THE BEATITUDES

Pilgrim, what is the Christian vision for the world?

The Christian vision for the world is one where God reigns in justice, peace and love.

....

How does Jesus Christ describe the citizens of God's kingdom?

Jesus said this to the crowds who followed him. They are known as the Beatitudes:

THE BEATITUDES

Blessed are the poor in spirit,
for theirs is the kingdom of heaven.

Blessed are those who mourn,
for they shall be comforted.

Blessed are the meek,
for they shall inherit the earth.

Blessed are those who hunger
and thirst after righteousness,
for they shall be satisfied.

Blessed are the merciful,
for they shall obtain mercy.

Blessed are the pure in heart,
or they shall see God.

Blessed are the peacemakers,
for they shall be called children of God.

Blessed are those who suffer
persecution for righteousness' sake,
for theirs is the kingdom of heaven.

What do we learn from these Beatitudes about the life of the kingdom?

We learn that we are blessed when we know our need of God, when we weep with compassion for the needs of the world, when we share God's longing for justice and peace, and when we clothe ourselves with mercy and grace.

What is the cost of the life of the kingdom?

Jesus Christ says that if any want to be his disciples, let them deny themselves, take up their cross daily and follow him.

What does it mean to carry the cross?

In baptism, Christians receive the sign of the
cross. We encourage one another to fight
valiantly against sin, the world and the devil,
and to remain faithful to Christ to the end of
our life.

....

What is the hope in which a Christian lives?

A Christian lives in the sure and certain hope
that as Jesus Christ rose from the dead,
so he will come again in glory to judge the
world. Christians believe that God will renew
the heavens and the earth, and that beyond
death we will enjoy eternal life with God.

Pilgrim, how will this shape the journey of your life?

I will seek to discover God's call on my life, use my gifts in God's service and share the way of Jesus Christ with others. By God's grace, I will live tomorrow's life today.